Costa Brava

Travel Guide

Quick Trips Series

Table of Contents

BUDGET TIPS 43

KNOW BEFORE YOU GO 56

Costa Brava

Located along the northeastern border of Spain, the

Costa Brava first rose to prominence as a tourist

destination during the 1950s. The name means "rugged

coast" in Spanish and the craggy rock formations on its

distinctive coastline could well have been sketched by one of the artists who call it home.

The lifestyle here is timeless and relatively unspoilt and there are plenty of sights and activities to amuse holidaymakers. Many towns and villages have retained charming medieval features. The area also includes the ruins of a Greek settlement over 2500 years old. Despite the region's popularity with tourists and the development of various resorts, remnants of the fishing villages of yesteryear endure to bridge the gap between old and new.

In more recent times, the region's beauty has played muse to a number of creative artists, novelists and poets, most notably the native-born Surrealist Salvador Dali. The

Dali Museum, conceived by the artist himself in the last decades of his life, is one of the most visited attractions in Spain.

There is more to the region than its rocky coastline. Where the Iberian Peninsula meets the Pyrenees Mountains, the Cap de Creus National Park features a rich diversity of geographical formations as well as plant and animal life. Aiguamolls de l'Empordà offers a fascinating glimpse into the life cycle of wetland creatures and La Garrotxa Volcanic Zone presents the opportunity to explore the impact of volcanic activity from Catalonia's past.

For sport lovers, Costa Brava offers a variety of water sport opportunities as well as several top-rated golf courses. A number of the Catalan beaches enjoy Blue Flag rating. There are several sites such as the Medes Islands, which are ideal for underwater exploration. If you are searching for a hip and vibrant nightlife, base yourself in Lloret de Mar. To immerse yourself in the visible remnants of various periods of the regions history, place Empuries, Pals, Tossa de Mar and Peratallada high on your itinerary.

Customs & Culture

Costa Brava comprises the coastal regions of Catalonia and the majority of the population is bilingual, with Catalonian being the native tongue. The region has a Mediterranean character and cosmopolitan atmosphere, thanks to trade relations that date back to 500 BC.

Evidence remain of both Greek and Roman colonies in the area.

Until the 1950s, however, Costa Brava attracted mainly local visitors and artists in search of inspiration. The best known figure representing the arts is without a doubt, Salvador Dali, a native of the region, but a number of other significant artists such as Joan Miró, as well as the author Quim Monzó, a well-known representative of the written word in Catalonian also found a home here. A somewhat surprising element of Costa Brava is the emergence of Americano Culture. This goes back to the 19th century, when a number of residents sought their fortune in the New World.

They may not have brought back ships of gold, but the influence of the Americas is unmistakable in the homes and other artwork they left. The style is particularly notable in the town of Begur.

The area hosts festivals dedicated to a large variety of music types, folk dancing, Habanera festivals and a variety of other cultural events, particularly in the spring and summer months.

🌏 Geography

Costa Brava is located along the northeastern coast of Spain, in the region of Catalonia and the province of Girona. The capital is also called Girona. It stretches from the mouth of the Tordera, near Blanes, to the border of France, with a small town called Portbou being its northernmost settlement. In between, the coastline dips and rises to create intriguing coves and impressive cliffs and crags.

The Costa Brava region is served by two airports in Girona and Barcelona. A railway line links Costa Brava with Southeast France, through the Portbou-Narbonne route and Spain via the Portbou-Barcelona line.

🌏 Weather & Best Time to Visit

The warmest months are July and August, reaching average highs around 27.5 degrees Celsius and night temperatures that remain warm around 20 degrees Celsius.

COSTA BRAVA TRAVEL GUIDE

May, September and October day temperatures can still reach the low to mid twenties, with the mercury dropping to just below the mid-teens at night. March, April and November sees a drop to between 14 and 17 degrees Celsius by day and night temperatures typically averaging around 7 to 9.5 degrees Celsius.

The highest rainfall figures can be expected in the months of May and September. Spring and autumn can see thunderstorms on Costa Brava. Frost occurs in winter, when night temperatures are known to drop as low as 2 or even 1 degree Celsius. Day temperatures of up to 12 to 13.5 degrees Celsius can be expected in the months of December and January.

Sights & Activities: What to See & Do

🌎 Blanes

Popularly referred to as the 'Gateway to Costa Brava', Blanes was first settled by the Romans in 300 BC. The town had fallen under Muslim and Christian rule, but saw large-scale destruction during the Catalan Revolt. A distinctive landmark, a rocky promontory named Sa Palomera, separates the more commercialized tourist section from the traditional fishing village.

This village is bounded on the other side by the harbor of Blanes. Fishing still plays an important part in the local economy. Another notable feature is the 15th century Gothic Fountain located at the old Blanes center. Featuring six waterspouts and decorated in a design that includes gargoyles as well as the heraldic emblems of the

Cabrera family, it was commissioned by Violant de Cabrera, daughter of the Count of Prades.

The town of Blanes has 4km's worth of beaches that carry Blue Flag rating, including S'Abanell, the longest beach on Costa Brava, which stretches for 2.1km from Plaça Del Països Catalans to the mouth of the Tordera River. At Playa Sabanell a variety of water activities such as fly-fishing, water skiing, wakeboarding and parasailing can be enjoyed. Beaches are well maintained and regularly re-sanded. The annual feast of Santa Anna and SantJoaquim in July coincides with an international fireworks competition that draws 500,000 visitors every year.

Botanical Gardens

Mar i Murtra

Passeig de Carles Faust, 9, 17300 Blanes

Tel.: 0034 972 330 826

Pinya de Rosa

Jardí Botànic Pinya de Rosa s/n, 17300 Blanes

Tel.: 0034 972 350 689

There are two gardens near Blanes worth a visit,

especially if you are interested in horticulture or botany.

The De Mar i Murtra Botanical Garden features a

collection of over 4000 plant species. The garden was

founded by the German Karl Faust and includes both

exotic and Mediterranean plants. It also offers a rare view

of Cala da Sa Forcanera beach, which can only be reached by sea.

Pinya de Rosa, which is located about 2km from Blanes, has 7000 different plant species. This tranquil garden was founded by the engineer Dr. FerranRiviere de Caralt in 1945 and features a particularly extensive collection of cacti as well as some unusual nocturnal flowers. This is one of the reasons why Pinya de Rosa is sometimes open till 8pm. Unfortunately the garden is not easily accessible via public transport.

Lloret de Mar

Formerly a fishing port, Lloret de Mar boasts a lively nightlife with around 30 night clubs and over 300 bars, as well as plenty of daily beach activities to amuse its visitors.

The town draws young adults and families, with attractions such as Water World, Gnomo Park, a theme park dedicated to gnomes and an aquatic zoo. Visitors seeking peace and quiet may appreciate a stroll through Santa Clotilde Garden, which blends the splendour of nature with a series of intriguing sculptures and offers beautiful views of the Mediterranean Sea, from its cliff top location.

Modernist Cemetery

Cami del Bon Repos,

Lloret de Mar, Spain

Tel:0034 972 365 788

The Age of Exploration prompted many persons of the Costa Brava to seek their fortunes in the Americas. Many returned unsuccessful, but what they did bring home with them, was a slightly different form of architectural and artistic expression. One of the places where this trend is evident is the Modernist Cemetery in Lloret de Mar.

Conceived by Joaquim Artau around 1896, the cemetery includes work by Josep Puig i Cadafalch, an architect responsible for several important buildings in Barcelona, Antoni M. Gallisà i Soqué, Lluís Llimona, Vicença Artigas I Albertí, Ismael Smith and the prominent modernist sculptor, Eusebi Arnau. Many of the artists were influenced by the work of Antoni Gaudí, a talented architect and important figure in the Catalan Modernist movement. The cemetery is regarded as one of the area's most important collections of funereal art.

🌏 Tossa de Mar

Tossa de Mar was first nudged into the public eye when the film 'Pandora and the Flying Dutchman' was released in 1951. It had been filmed around the town, and its female lead, Ava Gardner, won the hearts of locals.

The settlement dates back to Neolithic times. An early Iberian community made way for a Roman colony. In medieval times, the town fell under the administration of Barcelona, until it was ceded to the Abbot of Ripoll. Tossa de Mar gained autonomy during the 12th century. Fortification from the latter part of the Middle Ages remains one of Tossa de Mar's greatest attractions.

The beach area, Play Gran lies at the foot of these fortifications. A mere 600m, it is compact if compared to some of the other beach areas along Costa Brava. The promenade offers the usual water activities as well as plenty of bars and restaurants to relax and recharge.

Vila Vella

Despite withstanding raids from North Africa in the 15th century, the medieval fortification of Vila Vella, the Old Town of Tossa de Mar endure virtually intact into the 21st century. It provides a rare, living example of a walled medieval town that has stood the test of time. There are two gates in the wall, as well as seven defensive towers. Torre de lasHoras or the clock tower guarded the entry to the Patio de Armas or arsenal.

It is one of three cylindrical towers that have retained their original names. The other two are Torre d'en Joanàs, which overlooks the bay, and Torre del Codolar.

The earliest section of the city walls date back to the 12th and 13th century, but this was extended during the 14th century to include Torre de Can Magí. During the 15th century, at the height of African based pirate activity, these defences sheltered a community of eighty houses. One of the more striking features is the ruin of the Gothic church, església de Sant Vicenç. Constructed in the 15th century, this was blown up in the 19th century when the French used it to store explosives.

The site is occasionally used for concerts and other events. By night, the city walls are illuminated with special lighting. A relatively modern attraction within the Vila Vella section of Tossa de Mar is a sculpture of "Pandora", created by the artist CióAbellí and unveiled in 1998. The statue is not of the Pandora of myth, but honors the actress Ava Gardner, who starred in the 1951 movie *Pandora and the Flying Dutchman*, which was filmed on location around Tossa de Mar.

🌐 Peratallada & Pals (Windows on a Medieval Past)

Located 22km from Girona, Peratallada still retains some of its medieval features, in sections of fortification wall as well as a castle that dominates the landscape.

The original castle was partly damaged when besieged by Phillip III of France in 1285. It is fairly easy to distinguish between the older, more functional structure and the later style, which is more palatial in character. It included a prison, hospital and two towers. The castle now serves as hotel and restaurant. A moat surrounds the village, culminating in the Portal de la Virgen or the gateway of the Virgin. There are three other towers in the village, including the clock tower and a uniquely circular tower.

The town also has a 13th century Romanesque church, which is outside the Old Village and Place de les Voltes, the main square which is surrounded by medieval arcades. Peratallada is not far from the coastal town of Begur and the ruins at Empuries.

Another town well known for its medieval charm is Pals, with its distinctively cobbled streets and Gothic style features such as turrets and arches. It is a mere 5km from Peratallada and built on a hilltop. Some of the attractions include the Torre de les Hores or Tower of the Hours, a fine example of a Romanesque tower, the church of Sant Pere and a beautiful square, Placa Major. The town museum includes an authentic replica of an 18th century pharmacy as well as artefacts from an early 19th century English warship.

Sporting enthusiasts may be interested to know that there is a top rated golf course not far from Pals. Pals is located near the resort at Platja de Pals.

🌑 Diving in Costa Brava

There are several interesting diving sites on Costa Brava, most notably between L'Escala and L'Estartit. About 1km from the coast of L'Estartit, the Medes Islands present an unspoilt paradise of marine animal and plant life. There are also several shipwrecks off the coast between the two towns. Both L'Escala and L'Estartit have fully equipped diving centers.

Medes Islands

Just off the coast of Costa Brava near L'Estartit, diving enthusiasts will find a well-preserved marine wonderland at the Medes Islands. The famous French diver Jacques Cousteau documented his exploration of the area in 1955, and it has draws thousands of diving enthusiasts every year.

COSTA BRAVA TRAVEL GUIDE

The region is composed of seven uninhabited islands, various rocky cays, a selection of soft coral reefs and several underwater caves. Nutrient-rich currents ensure an abundance of marine life, while the rock formations offer breathtaking underwater scenery.

The best-known demarcated diving area is Dolphin Cave, a huge chamber which features various chimneys and windows that filter in sunlight. Other notable diving spots include Medallot and Meda Gran. As the area is protected, the fish have become fairly tame and accustomed to human intrusions. A festival showcasing the best of underwater photography takes place in the Medes Islands in the beginning of June.

Shipwrecks

There are several shipwrecks worth exploring between L'Escala and L'Estartit. The Reggio Messina is the largest of these at 115m. Formerly a transport ferry, it was deliberately sunk in 1991. Considerably smaller at 47m, the Avenire, also known as the Marmoler, was wrecked in a storm in 1971. Still mostly intact, the wreck has become home to a vibrant ecosystem of marine life. The Constantine ran aground on a small island, IllaMateau, which is located off L'Escala. Accessible from the beach, this is a shallow dive, but features a great opportunity to view its marine life.

A little further from the L'Escala region, two wartime casualties can be explored. Saint Prosper, a 106m-cargo ship went down in the Bay of Roses after colliding with a floating mine. An excursion can be organized through the diving centers of L'Escala and Roses. An earlier wreck, from the First World War, can be found in the bay of EsCaials, off Cadaques, to the north. This is a British vessel, the Llanishen, which was torpedoed by the Germans. To explore the Llanishen, you will need to contact the Cadaques Diving Center.

🌐 L'Escala

Located at the southern end of the Bay of Roses, L'Escala features several Blue Flag beaches and the enigmatic ancient ruins at Empuries.

The town offers facilities for a number of sporting activities such as golf, horse riding, cycling, tennis and go carting, as well as a number of water-based sports such as kayaking, snorkelling, fishing and sailing. The town is well known for its anchovies and hosts an annual festival to honor this. The Old Town and Promenade regions are popular locations for casual exploring and additionally, the Promenade becomes the setting for a weekly market on Sundays.

Empuries

Empuries offers the opportunity to view remnants from various styles of past civilization within close proximity of each other. The archaeological site itself contains layers of Greek and Roman artifacts. The Greek colony, originally named Emporion or "market" developed out of regular trade between the local settlers and Greek merchants.

An initial settlement on a small island in the Fluvià river mouth expanded over time to the mainland and Empuries grew to become the largest Greek colony in Iberia. A new chapter opened when Carthagian hostilities moved the Roman military leader, Gnaeus Cornelius Scipio to occupy the site around 215 BC. By the time of Emperor Augustus, the Greek and Roman settlements had unified. Between 200 and 300 AD, the first Christian evangelists reached its shores, but Viking raids led to a gradual period of decline during the early Middle Ages.

Modern excavation began around 1908 under Emili Gandia i Ortega and Josep Puig i Cadafalch, and continue to this day. Still visible at the dig, are features such as an enormous Roman wall and an impressive water purification system, as well as paintings and mosaics. The layout of the forum and the amphitheatre is clearly visible and the temple includes a sculpture of Asclepios, Greek god of Medicine. The museum exhibits individual artefacts that have been uncovered such as ceramics, sculptures, tools and utensils. Only a small portion of the settlement has so far been uncovered.

Empuriabrava

With more than 40km worth of canals and a seasonal population of up to 80,000, residents, Empuriabrava could almost be likened to a large town or small city on the water. It is one of the largest marinas in the world. Located on a wetland, the area was developed between the mid-1960s to mid-1970s. The nearby aerodrome has a flight school and also offers skydiving. The area offers a wide variety of water sport and opportunities for boat rental at various levels. One distinctive landmark is the club Nautic Tower.

Castelló d'Empúries

Castellód'Empúries was once the capital of the county of Empúries, but it has in recent years been dwarfed by the rapid development of the Empuriabrava. The town is located halfway between Figueres and Roses and at the mouth of the Muga River.

Its primary landmark is the church of Santa Maria, a fine example of Gothic architecture, which dates back to the 15th century. Some of its features include the high altar with detailed artwork by Vicenç Borràs and a huge 18th century Baroque organ. In September, the town becomes the setting for a medieval festival.

🌐 La Garrotxa Volcanic Zone

Although the last volcanic activity in the La Garrotxa Volcanic Zone occurred at least 11,000 years ago, the National Park still bears many reminders of the event and others even further back in history. There are around 40 volcano cones and 28 lava flows to observe, some of which have remained quite well preserved. The volcanic field is termed as monogenetic, meaning that its features were created by single cataclysmic events, rather than a series of eruptions.

The tallest volcano in the region is Volcan Croscat. Its height is a relatively modest 160m. Dated at between 12,000 and 15,000 years old, it is also relatively young, but quite well preserved. The formation clearly shows the paths of various flows of lava.

The La Garrotxa Volcanic Natural Park has 28 different walking routes, most of which are clearly sign-posted. The vegetation is quite lush, but since the majority of the park is on private land, visitors should avoid disturbing the plant and animal life. There are demarcated rest areas, which should preferably be used for picnicking.

The area can also be explored on horseback, via a bicycle route, from a tourist train or a hot air balloon. La Garrotxa Volcanic Zone is located on the road towards Olot, and can best be reached by rented car, taxi or via a bus service from Olot.

🌐 Figueres

The town of Figueres evolved from the remnants of two Roman settlements, Juncària and Figàries, but it first began to show some growth during the 10th century. The town's economy was considerably boosted by the construction of the SantFerran castle, for which it became a supply station. Most tourists, however, are drawn to Figueres, to view the works and landmarks associated with Salvador Dali, the town's most famous citizen. The Old Town and Plaça de les Patates retain some of its original charm and character. The town is named for the fig trees that thrive in great abundance within the region.

Teatro Museo Dali

Gala-Salvador Dalí Square, 5, E-17600 Figueres

Tel: 0034 972 677 500

The Surrealist painter Salvador Dali was larger than life and his eccentric attitude is remembered as much in his flamboyant appearance and lifestyle as in the unusual art he left behind in the galleries of the world. The artist was born in Figueres, but also spent much time at Cadaques, where his family had a summer home.

He received the earliest portion of his art education in Figueres, where he also had his first exhibition.

Dali incorporated a variety of influences into his work, but owed a particular debt to another Catalonian artist Joan Miro, who played some role in introducing Dali to surrealism. After several years in the USA, Dali returned to Catalonia and in 1960 began the creation of the

DalíTeatroMuseo in Figueres. This was first opened to the public in 1974.

The Dali TeatroMuseo is a must-see for anyone remotely interested in the artist or his work. Not only does Dali lie buried in its crypt, but it also occupies the exact location of his debut exhibition and is within a stone's throw of the house where he was born and the church where he was baptized.

The TeatroMuseo Dali is an experiment in perception and contains and utilizes a vast selection of media. The Mae West room features a living room, which had been furnished to display a three-dimensional likeness of the Hollywood actress Mae West's face, when viewed from a certain position. It is based on a painting, "Ilvolto di Mae West", that was completed around 1935.

The museum also features a modest collection of art by others that Dali had owned. These include works by El Greco, the Dadaist Marcel Duchamp and AntoniPitxot, who had been a personal friend of Dali.

Sant Ferran Castle

http://www.castillosanfernando.org/

Near Figueres, you will find an important castle of Catalonia, the SantFerran castle, which dates back to the second half of the 17th century. At the time, there were frequent border incidents with France and fortification was necessary for defensive purposes.

Designed by Don Juan Martín Zermeño, then the Commandant-in-Chief of the Engineering Corps, the structure featured a double ring of ramparts and had barracks to accommodate 6000 men and 500 horses. Its cistern had the capacity to hold around 40 million litres of water. It covers 32.5 acres of ground and the moat is 5km in length. The pentagon-shaped castle is located on a hill that overlooks Figueres. These days the setting is mostly used for events such as horse shows and music concerts.

🌐 Aiguamolls de l'Empordà

Another attraction of the Bay of Roses is the Aiguamolls de l'Empordà National Park, a wetland located between the Muga and Fluvià River. Comprising an extensive network of pastures, marshes and canals of brackish water, it is home to over 300 species of water birds and other wildlife. These include the Great Spotted Cuckoo, the spoonbill, the Stone Curlew, the Nightingale, the flamenco, Audouin's gull, the osprey and the Collared Pratincole. Colonies of White Stork and Purple Gallinule have been re-introduced to the region.

The bird life features species that breed in the area as well as those who only use the area as a stop in their seasonal migration. Other fauna include palmate and marbled newts, various types of frogs and snakes, the European pond terrapin and also fallow deer and polecats. There is an observation tower for bird watchers as well as a special track for visitors who are wheelchair bound. The Aiguamolls de l'Empordà National Park is located on the road towards Sant Pere Pescador.

🌐 Girona

Girona has retained much of its medieval features.

Particularly memorable are the stone steps and narrow

cobbled streets of what was once the Jewish Quarter.

Equally picturesque is one of the oldest sections of the

city, the RiuOnyar riverside, which presents a cluttered,

but colorful patchwork of buildings.

A prominent landmark is the Cathedral of Saint Mary of

Girona, a building completed to its present form over a

two hundred year period between the 11th and the 13th

century. It combines Romanesque and Gothic features. In

Sant Pere, near the town wall and the cathedral, you will

also find the John Lennon Gardens, a tranquil park that

was named by a past mayor to honor his favourite

musician. The city has several museums worth a visit.

These include the Museum of the Cinema, the Girona Art Museum and the Museum of Jewish History.

Jewish Quarter

Calle de la Forca,

Girona, Spain

As a community, the Jews endured complex and complicated relationships with both Christians and Muslims. Nowhere was this more evident than in Spain, where the Jews generally enjoyed better status and prospects under Moorish rule. For the Jews, the final stages of the Reconquesta of Spain brought a difficult choice of exile or enduring religious persecution.

Prior to the departure of Spain's Jewish community, Girona had been home to a large and prosperous Jewish Quarter. Calle de la Força has since Roman times the main street of this neighborhood and a venue of brisk trade. Some of the past is recaptured in the Museum of Jewish History, which provides an informative introduction and guide to a vanished community.

Sant Pere de Rodes

El Port de la Selva,

Girona, Spain

TheSant Pere de Rodes monastery is located on the mountain of Verdera and overlooks the Mediterranean Sea. Along the curving road towards the monastery, dolmans and other Megalithic features can be seen. The

COSTA BRAVA TRAVEL GUIDE

structure itself is considered one of the oldest religious buildings in the province of Catalonia, its true origins unknown.

Historical records first make mention of a religious cell dedicated to St Peter in 878, but it may have been a modest community until 945, when it was reputedly founded as a Benedictine monastery, under a separate abbot. It rose to the height of its prominence during the 11th and 12th century. The 12th century bell tower is in the Lombardy Romanesque style.

The building was repeated looted during the 18th century, which ultimately led to it being abandoned. The monastery has an austere, but timeless beauty. These days the building serves as a museum. An information sheet will guide you through a numbered tour. Above the monastery, the ruins of Castello de Sant Salvador can be reached after a steep 25-minute hike.

Cadaques

To the east of Figueres lies Cadaques, another town that played a part in the life of Salvador Dali. Located on a bay of the Cap de Creus Peninsula, it had once been a modest fishing village. The area is characterized by spectacular and somewhat unusual rock formations. Although not an island, these impressive rocks have played a role of isolating the town from its surroundings, circumstances that played has played a role in the preservation of an older form of the Catalan dialect amongst its residents.

COSTA BRAVA TRAVEL GUIDE

The remoteness has drawn a number of other artistic souls to the region, ranging from Picasso and Miro to Walt Disney and Alfred Hitchcock, as well as Dadaists like Man Ray and Marcel Duchamp.

As the result, you can expect the unusual and the slightly eccentric to express itself in the shops and architecture of Cadaques. There are several craft shops and galleries worth exploring near the Plaza Mayor. Do pay a visit to Salvador Dali's home, now also a museum, which is at Port Lligat.

Portbou

Portbou is the last town of Costa Brava before the border with France is reached. It boasts a population of barely more than 1300 people. The Hotel de Francia is known as the site where the fleeing German Jewish philosopher Walter Benjamin committed suicide rather than being repatriated back into German hands. A memorial, entitled 'Passages' was created in his honor on a cliff by the town cemetery. There are various facets to the monument, as visitors descend down a tunnel to reach a glass window, which offers a view of the whirling sea currents below. The memorial is the work of an Israeli artist, DaniKaravanhe.

The town is a railway junction, which connects the Barcelona-Portbou line from Spain with the Narbonne-Portbou network from France, as trains have to change from the Standard Gauge to Iberian Gauge railways, via a variable gauge system. During the Spanish Civil War, the town also served as a major supply base for the

Republican side.

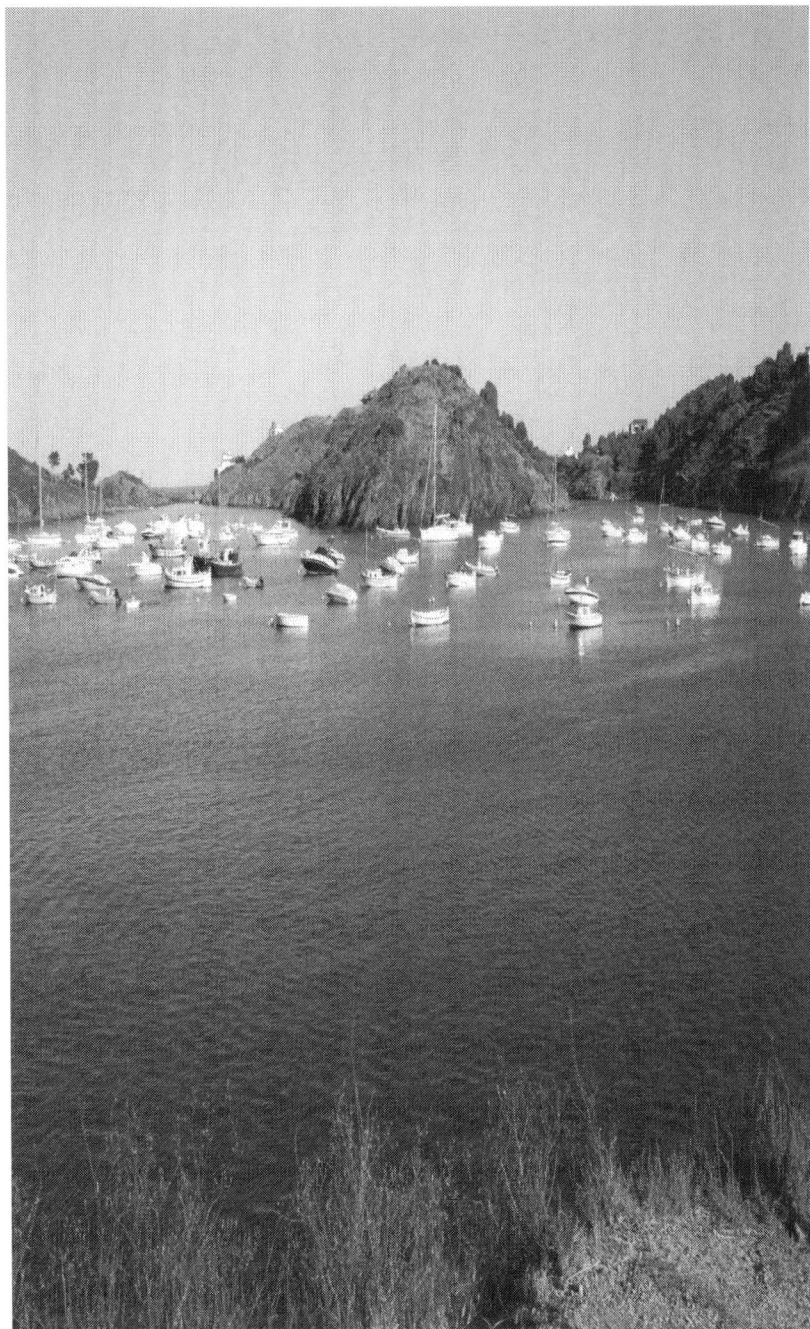

Budget Tips

🌐 Accommodation

Hotel Costabella

Avenida de Francia 61, 17007 Girona, Spain

Tel:0034 972 202 524

http://hotelcostabella.com/

The Hotel Costabella is located on the outskirts of Girona, but compensates with its affordable rates. There is a fitness center, which includes sauna and hydro-massage services, a swimming pool, a business center, a restaurant and free Wifi Internet. The downstairs lounge offers games and television. The hotel is wheel chair friendly and the rooms are spacious and comfortable.

Hotel staff members are friendly and efficient.

Accommodation begins at €40 which includes breakfast.

Hotel Mercedes

Avda Frederic Mistral 32, 17310 Lloret de Mar, Spain

http://www.hotelmercedes.com/

Hotel Mercedes is located 500m from the beach and 300m from the center of town and offers a friendly family setting with plenty of character. The hotel has a bar, sauna and swimming pool, as well as two dining rooms. Rooms include central heating and air conditioning, bath and shower facilities and satellite TV. A safety box is an optional extra that is charged separately. Wifi Internet is free. Accommodation begins at €31 and includes breakfast.

Hotel Samba

C/ Francesc Cambo 10, 17310 Lloret de Mar, Spain

Hotel Samba is located 10 minutes away from Fenals Beach. The hotel has a business center, a swimming pool, a lounge bar and a restaurant. There are also facilities for tennis and golf. Rooms include central heating, air-conditioning, a private bathroom and satellite TV. There are special conveniences for the disabled. Staff members are helpful and relatively fluent in English. Accommodation begins at €45 and includes breakfast. There is an option of all-inclusive full board, which covers all meals and drinks.

Hotel Oasis Tossa

Lope Mateo 3, 17320 Tossa de Mar, Spain

Tel: 00 34 972 34 07 50

Hotel Oasis Tossa is located within easy strolling distance from the Old Town and the beach. The hotel has a restaurant, fitness center, a sauna, games room, bar, spa, hydro-massage service, an indoor and outdoor swimming pool, Internet services and wheelchair friendly facilities. Rooms include air-conditioning, bathroom, television and hairdryer, as well as an electronic locking system. A mini-fridge and a safe are optional extras that are charged separately. Accommodation begins at €64 and includes breakfast as well as the resort fee.

Hotel Stella Maris

Av Vila de Madrid 18, 17300 Blanes, Spain

Hotel Stella Maris is located near the beaches, but about a 20-minute stroll from the town center and the Promenade. The hotel has tennis courts, a swimming pool, and a restaurant and offers free high-speed Internet. The hotel staff members are described as friendly, helpful and attentive and rooms include air-conditioning, en-suite bathroom and satellite TV. Accommodation begins at €37 per night and includes breakfast.

🌐 Restaurants, Cafés & Bars

Café Terrassans

Passeig de Dintre 31,

17300 Blanes, Catalonia, Spain

Tel: 0034 972 330 081

Café Terrassans is an authentic tapas bar, located within the Old Village of Blanes. Named after the Farm Workers Union, which used to occupy one of the rooms above the bar, the friendly, relaxed atmosphere makes it a firm favourite with locals as well as visitors. Available items are listed on the blackboard and these may include garlic prawns, calamaresallaromana, fried cuttlefish and meatballs. The seafood dishes are freshly caught and prepared. The food is very reasonably priced. Expect to pay between €5.50 and €12.

Bahiton

Peixateries, 1, Tossa de Mar, Spain

Tel: 0034 972 341 435

Bahiton is a small, family-run restaurant with a reputation for a great selection in Spanish style cuisine and an authentic local ambiance.

Seafood features prominently on the menu with dishes such as a mixed seafood grill, grilled sardines, mussels in tomato sauce and red peppers stuffed with salt cod, but there are other choices such as warm goats cheese salad, meat kebabs and many more. Expect to pay around €17.50 per person. As a firm favourite with locals, the restaurant is always busy.

Restaurante Duran

Calle Lasauca, 5,

17600 Figueres, Spain

COSTA BRAVA TRAVEL GUIDE

Tel: 0034 972 501 250

Most people visit Figueres to view Dali's famous Teatro Museum and Restaurant Duran presents an excellent opportunity to soak up a little more of the Surreal. The decor includes plenty of photographs of the flamboyant artist.

The building dates to 1855 and the restaurant was frequented by Dali himself. Some of the menu highlights include hare loin with chestnut puree and raspberry sauce, Monkfish medallions with shrimp and clams prepared Cadaqués style, Paella with lobster, chicken croquettes, langoustines with lemon hollandaise, and sole in orange sauce. Expect to pay around €20 for a three-course meal.

Blue Sky Lounge Bar

Sector San Maurici, 347, Empuriabrava, Spain

Tel: 0034 972 450 281

After having feasted your eyes on the Venice of Costa Brava, let your taste buds have their turn at the Blue Sky Lounge Bar. The menu is creative, attractively presented and changes regularly. Expect unlikely combinations such as chouriza and clams, chicken salad with pear, walnut and port wine, penne with salmon and vodka and baked hake with clams, garlic, parsley, tomatoes and potatoes. Dessert options include tiramisu and ice cream. A three-course meal would cost €15 for lunch and €18 for dinner.

Giorgio Restaurant

Avinguda de la Mare de Deu de Gracia, 21,

Lloret de Mar, Spain

Giorgio serves pasta, homemade pizza, seafood and tenderly grilled steaks. Some of the menu items include Andalusian Salad with avo and shrimp and lobster with rice. Service is efficient and the restaurant boasts an extensive wine selection. Expect to pay between €30 and €35 for a three-course meal.

Shopping

Something to bear in mind when shopping Costa Brava, is that many shops close in the afternoon between 2pm and 5m, but stay open until about 8pm in the evening.

La Bisbal d'Emporda

La Bisbal d'Empordà tourist office

Tel.: 0034 972 645 166

Located 29km southeast of Girona, the town La Bisbal is

famous for the quality of its pottery and cermamics, which

constitutes a major portion of the local economy.

The crafting of clay goes back generations, in many of the

towns families. Most of the town's shops display some

form of pottery, whether it takes the shape of huge

flowerpots or vases, colored tiles or sculpted figurines.

The emphasis is firmly on decorative art, but different

outlets focus their efforts on different sections of the

market.

Manufacturers with a more artistic approach include Cerámicas Torres (Tel: 972 644 004), Lluís Puigdemont (Tel: 972 643 916), Marchos Pacheco (Tel: 620 299 511) and Rogenca Ceramista (Tel: 972 640 840). For garden related items, visit Ceràmica La Estrella (Tel: 972 643 414) at Avda.

Parallel 52 and if you are looking for items that combine the decorative with the functional, do stop at Ceràmica Artesanal Puigdemont (Tel: 972 640 425) on C/ de la Indústria 17. The town has a museum, which is located in the old pottery factory as well as a School of Pottery.

Shopping in Girona

For handmade chocolate, try Cacao Sampaka at CalleSta Clara 45. Chocolate is combined with a variety of traditional and more unusual fillings. Ambrosia at c/Careras Peralta 4 sells the produce of monks and nuns, with a theme that is distinctly medieval.

These include herbal remedies and homemade biscuits, but also ancient devotional music on CD, maps, miniatures and enamelled goods. Faure at Carrer de l'Argenteria 25 sells handcrafted chocolate including chocolate flies. The flies have a special meaning in Girona. They commemorate a local legend about French troops being defeated by a swarm of flies that emerged from the grave of Saint Narcissus. Colmado Moriscot at C/ Ciutadans 4, stocks a variety of traditional food items and delicatessen. The shop was founded in 1908, and still uses a vintage brass cash register from that era. For gifts, visit Nou Taller de Vidre (0034 972 416 330) at Carrer

Hortes 2, a shop that specializes in glass art and includes

jewellery and textiles in its uniquely crafted items.

Markets in Costa Brava

Most of the towns of Costa Brava have a weekly market,

which may sell food and fresh produce, but also crafts

and other goods. Girona's market is at Parc de la Devesa

on Tuesdays and Saturdays and trades in crafts, clothing

and food items. In Figueres, the weekly market happens

on Thursdays and this includes fresh produce and craft

items.

Visit Blanes on Mondays to take part in the trading of

clothes, household items and souvenirs at Passeig de

Mar. There are street markets in Lloret de Mar, Pals and

Palamos on Tuesdays, in SantAntoni de Calonge on

Wednesdays, Calonge and L'Estartit on Thursdays and

La Bisbal and Platjad'Aro on Fridays.

Shopping in Pals

The medieval town of Pals has a number of craft outlets.

Pottery features prominently. CeramicaPlanas Marques

(Tel: 972 636 402) on Plaza Mayor 8 trades in ceramics.

La Torre de les Hores Antique (972 63 60 72) specializes

in toys, antiques, boxes and other collectibles, often

lovingly restored by the owner. Jaaba Art and Fashion

(Tel: 972 63 64 54) features a variety of colorful and

original designs in clothing, jewellery and other

keepsakes.

Another shop selling fashion and wearable art is Embolic,

Fashion and Jewels en Pals (Tel: 972 66 78 60). Leather

Yoli (Tel: 972 63 62 43) has a leather workshop at C/ Vinyers, 6. Pals RS (Tel: 972 66 80 92) is a souvenir and wine shop, located at Plaza Mayor 6. Stop here for postcards and other small gifts.

Shopping in Cadaques

Cadaques is somewhat remote from the rest of Costa Brava, due to its unusual geography, but if you should take a trip to the town, you will be rewarded with a range of original and highly creative shops unrivalled by the rest of Costa Brava. Eleet Mo on RibaPoal features clothing and accessories in a retro sixties hippy style, while La Pepa (Tel: 0034 972159231) on Port-alguer features a slightly more exclusive and stylish alternative. Fans of Indian culture will enjoy Moksha, a shop that features clothing as well as Hindu type jewellery and emblems.

Moksha (0034 696613776) can be found at Pl. del

Estrella.

Know Before You Go

🌐 Entry Requirements

By virtue of the Schengen agreement, visitors from other countries in the European Union will not need a visa when visiting Spain. Additionally visitors from Switzerland, Norway, Lichtenstein, Iceland, Canada, the United Kingdom, Australia and the USA are also exempt. Independently travelling minors will need to carry written permission from their parents. If visiting from a country where you require a visa to enter Spain, you will also need to state the purpose of your visit and provide proof that you have financial means to support yourself for the duration of your stay. Unless you are an EU national, your passport should be valid for at least 3 months after the end of your stay.

🌐 Health Insurance

Citizens of other EU countries are covered for emergency health care in Spain. UK residents, as well as visitors from Switzerland are covered by the European Health Insurance Card (EHIC), which can be applied for free of charge. Visitors from non-Schengen countries will need to show proof of private health insurance that is valid for the duration of their stay in Spain, as part of their visa application.

🌎 Travelling with Pets

Spain participates in the Pet Travel Scheme (PETS) which allows UK residents to travel with their pets without requiring quarantine upon re-entry. Certain conditions will need to be met. The animal will have to be microchipped and up to date on rabies vaccinations. Additionally, you will need a PETS re-entry certificate issued by a UK vet, an Export Health Certificate (this is required by the Spanish authorities), an official Certificate of Treatment against dangerous parasites such as tapeworm and ticks and an official Declaration that your pet has not left the qualifying countries within this period. Pets from the USA or Canada may be brought in under the conditions of a non-commercial import. For this, your pet will also need to be microchipped (or marked with an identifying tattoo) and up to date on rabies vaccinations.

🌎 Airports

Adolfo Suárez Madrid–Barajas Airport (MAD) is the largest and busiest airport in Spain. It is located about 9km from the financial district of Madrid, the capital. The busiest route is the so-called "Puente Aéreo" or "air bridge", which connects Madrid with Barcelona. The second busiest airport in Spain is **Barcelona–El Prat Airport** (BCN), located about 14km southwest from the center of Barcelona. There are two terminals. The newer Terminal 1 handles the bulk of its traffic, while the older Terminal 2 is used by budget airlines such as EasyJet.

Palma de Mallorca Airport (PMI) is the third largest airport in Spain and one of its busiest in the summer time. It has the capacity of processing 25 million passengers annually. **Gran Canaria Airport** (LPA) handles around 10 million passengers annually and connects travellers with the Canary Islands. **Pablo Ruiz Picasso Malaga Airport** (AGP) provides access to the Costa del Sol. Other southern airports are **Seville Airport** (SVQ), **Jaen Federico Garcia Lorca Airport** (GRX) near Granada, **Jerez de la Frontera Airport**, which connects travellers to Costa del Luz and Cadiz and **Almeria Airport** (LEI).

🌏 Airlines

Iberia is the flag carrying national airline of Spain. Since a merger in 2010 with British Airways, it is part of the International Airlines Group (IAG). Iberia is in partnership with the regional carrier Air Nostrum and Iberia Express, which focusses on medium and short haul routes. Vueling is a low-cost Spanish airline with connections to over 100 destinations. In partnership with MTV, it also provides a seasonal connection to Ibiza. Volotea is a budget airline based in Barcelona, which mainly flies to European destinations. Air Europe, the third largest airline after Iberia and Vueling connects Europe to resorts in the Canaries and the Balearic Islands and also flies to North and South America. Swiftair flies mainly to destinations in Europe, North Africa and the Middle East.

Barcelona-El Prat Airport serves as a primary hub for Iberia Regional. It is also a hub for Vueling. Additionally it functions as a regional hub for Ryanair. Air Europe's primary hubs are at Palma de Mallorca Airport and Madrid Barajas Airport, but other bases are at Barcelona Airport and Tenerife South Airport. Air Nostrum is served by hubs at Barcelona Airport, Madrid Barajas Airport and Valencia Airport. Gran Canaria Airport is the hub for the regional airline, Binter Canarias.

Currency

Spain's currency is the Euro. It is issued in notes in denominations of €500, €200, €100, €50, €20, €10 and €5. Coins are issued in denominations of €2, €1, 50c, 20c, 10c, 5c, 2c and 1c.

🌐 Banking & ATMs

You should have no trouble making withdrawals in Spain if your ATM card is compatible with the MasterCard/Cirrus or Visa/Plus networks. If you want to save money, avoid using the dynamic currency conversion (DCC) system, which promises to charge you in your own currency for the Euros you withdraw. The fine print is that your rate will be less favorable. Whenever possible, opt to conduct your transaction in Euros instead. Do remember to advise your bank or credit card company of your travel plans before leaving.

🌐 Credit Cards

Visa and MasterCard will be accepted at most outlets that handle credit cards in Spain, but you may find that your American Express card is not as welcome at all establishments. While shops may still be able to accept transactions with older magnetic strip cards, you will need a PIN enabled card for transactions at automatic vendors such as ticket sellers. Do not be offended when asked to show proof of ID when paying by credit card. It is common practice in Spain and Spaniards are required by law to carry identification on them at all times.

🌐 Tourist Taxes

In the region of Catalonia, which includes Barcelona, a tourist tax of between €0.45 and €2.50 per night is levied for the first seven days of your stay. The amount depends on the standard of the establishment, but includes youth hostels, campgrounds, holiday apartments and cruise ships with a stay that exceeds 12 hours.

🌐 Reclaiming VAT

If you are not from the European Union, you can claim back VAT (or Value Added Tax) paid on your purchases in Spain. The VAT rate in Spain is 18 percent. VAT refunds are made on purchases of €90.15 and over from a single shop. Look for shops displaying Global Blue Tax Free Shopping signage. You will be required to fill in a form at the shop, which must then be stamped at the Customs office at the airport. Customs officers will want to inspect your purchases to make sure that they are sealed and unused. Once this is done, you will be able to claim your refund from the Refund Office at the airport. Alternately, you can mail the form to Global Blue once you get home for a refund on your credit card.

🌐 Tipping policy

In general, Spain does not really have much of a tipping culture and the Spanish are not huge tippers themselves. When in a restaurant, check your bill to see whether a gratuity is already included. If not, the acceptable amount will depend on the size of the meal, the prestige of the restaurant and the time of day. For a quick coffee, you can simply round the amount off. For lunch in a modest establishment, opt for 5 percent or one euro per person. The recommended tip for dinner would be more generous, usually somewhere between 7 and 10 percent. This will depend on the type of establishment.

In hotels, if there is someone to help you with your luggage, a tip of 1 euro should be sufficient. At railway stations and airports, a tip is not really expected. Rounding off the amount of the fare to the nearest euro would be sufficient for a taxi driver. If you recruited a private driver, you may wish to tip that person at the end of your association with him.

🌐 Mobile Phones

Most EU countries, including Spain uses the GSM mobile service. This means that most UK phones and some US and Canadian phones and mobile devices will work in Spain. While you could check with your service provider about coverage before you leave, using your own service in roaming mode will involve additional costs. The alternative is to purchase a Spanish SIM card to use during your stay in Spain.

Spain has four mobile networks. They are Movistar, Vodafone, Orange and Yoiga. Buying a Spanish SIM card is relatively simple and inexpensive. By law, you will be required to show some form of identification such as a passport. A basic SIM card from Vodafone costs €5. There are two tourist packages available for €15, which offers a combination of 1Gb data, together with local and international call time. Alternately, a data only package can also be bought for €15. From Orange, you can get a SIM card for free, with a minimum top-up purchase of €10. A tourist SIM with a combination of data and voice calls can be bought for €15. Movistar offers a start-up deal of €10. At their sub-branches, Tuenti, you can also get a free SIM, but the catch is that you need to choose a package to get it. The start-up cost at Yoiga is €20.

🌐 Dialling Code

The international dialling code for Spain is +34.

🌐 Emergency Numbers

All Emergencies: 112 (no area code required)

Police (municipal): 092

Police (national): 091

Police (tourist police, Madrid): 91 548 85 37

Police (tourist police, Barcelona): 93 290 33 27

Ambulance: 061 or 112

Fire: 080 or 112

Traffic: 900 123 505

Electricity: 900 248 248

Immigration: 900 150 000

MasterCard: 900 958 973

Visa: 900 99 1124

🌐 Public Holidays

1 January: New Year's Day (Año Nuevo)

6 January: Day of the Epiphany/Three Kings Day (Reyes Mago)

March/April: Good Friday

1 May: Labor Day (Día del Trabajo)

15 August: Assumption of Mary (Asunción de la Virgen)

12 October: National Day of Spain/Columbus Day (Fiesta Nacional de España or Día de la Hispanidad)

1 November: All Saints Day (Fiesta de Todos los Santos)

6 December: Spanish Constitution Day (Día de la Constitución)

8 December: Immaculate Conception (La Immaculada)

25 December: Christmas (Navidad)

Easter Monday is celebrated in the Basque region, Castile-La Mancha, Catalonia, La Rioja, Navarra and Valencia. 26 December is celebrated as Saint Stephen's Day in Catalonia and the Balearic Islands.

🌍 Time Zone

Spain falls in the Central European Time Zone. This can be calculated as Greenwich Mean Time/Co-ordinated Universal Time (GMT/UTC) +2; Eastern Standard Time (North America) -6; Pacific Standard Time (North America) -9.

🌍 Daylight Savings Time

Clocks are set forward one hour on the last Sunday in March and set back one hour on the last Sunday in October for Daylight Savings Time.

🌐 School Holidays

Spain's academic year is from mid-September to mid-June. It is divided into three terms with two short breaks of about two weeks around Christmas and Easter.

🌐 Trading Hours

Trading hours in Spain usually run from 9.30am to 1.30pm and from 4.30pm to 8pm, from Mondays to Saturdays. Malls and shopping centers often trade from 10am to 9pm without closing. During the peak holiday seasons, shops could stay open until 10pm. Lunch is usually served between 1pm and 3.30pm while dinner is served from 8.30 to 11pm.

🌐 Driving Laws

The Spanish drive on the right hand side of the road. You will need a driver's licence which is valid in the EC to be able to hire a car in Spain. The legal driving age is 18, but most rental companies will require you to be at least 21 to be able to rent a car. You will need to carry your insurance documentation and rental contract with you at all times, when driving. The speed limit in Spain is 120km per hour on motorways, 100km per hour on dual carriageways and 90km per hour on single carriageways. Bear in mind that it is illegal to drive in Spain wearing sandals or flip-flops.

You may drive a non-Spanish vehicle in Spain provided that it is considered roadworthy in the country where it is registered. As a UK resident, you will be able to drive a vehicle registered in the UK in Spain for up to six months, provided that your liabilities as a UK motorist, such as MOT, road tax and insurance are up to date for the entire period of your stay. The legal limit in Spain is 0.05, but for new drivers who have had their licence for less than two years, it is 0.03.

🌍 Drinking Laws

In Spain, the minimum drinking age is 18. Drinking in public places is forbidden and can be punished with a spot fine. In areas where binge drinking can be a problem, alcohol trading hours are often limited.

🌍 Smoking Laws

In the beginning of 2006, Spain implemented a policy banning smoking from all public and private work places. This includes schools, libraries, museums, stadiums, hospitals, cinemas, theatres and shopping centers as well as public transport. From 2011, smoking was also banned in restaurants and bars, although designated smoking areas can be created provided they are enclosed and well ventilated. Additionally tobacco products may only be sold from tobacconists and bars and restaurants where smoking is permitted. Smoking near children's parks, schools or health centers carries a €600 fine.

Electricity

Electricity: 220 volts

Frequency: 50 Hz

Your electrical appliances from the UK and Ireland should be able to function sufficiently in Spain, but since Spain uses 2 pin sockets, you will need a C/F adapter to convert the plug from 3 to 2-pins. The voltage and frequency is compatible with UK appliances. If travelling from the USA, you will need a converter or step-down transformer to convert your appliances to 110 volts. The latest models of many laptops, camcorders, cell phones and digital cameras are dual-voltage with a built in converter.

Food & Drink

Spanish cuisine is heavily influenced by a Moorish past. Staple dishes include the rice dish, Paella, Jamon Serrano (or Spanish ham), Gazpacho (cold tomato-based vegetable soup), roast

COSTA BRAVA TRAVEL GUIDE

suckling pig, chorizo (spicy sausage) and the Spanish omelette. Tapas (hot or cold snacks) are served with drinks in Spanish bars.

The most quintessentially Spanish drink is sangria, but a popular alternative with the locals is tinto de verano, or summer wine, a mix of red wine and lemonade. Vino Tinto or red wine compliments most meal choices. The preferred red grape type is Tempranillo, for which the regions of Roija and Ribera del Duero are famous. A well-known sparkling wine, Cava, is grown in Catalonia. Do try the Rebujito, a Seville style mix of sherry, sparkling water and mint. The most popular local beers are Cruzcampo, Alhambra and Estrello Damm. Coffee is also popular with Spaniards, who prefer Café con leche (espresso with milk).

Websites

http://www.idealspain.com
A detailed resource that includes legal information for anyone planning a longer stay or residency in Spain.
http://spainattractions.es/
http://www.tourspain.org/
http://spainguides.com/
http://www.travelinginspain.com/
http://wikitravel.org/en/Spain

Printed in Great Britain
by Amazon